C000184732

Moving on Up

Secrets to an Upbeat and Happy Life

By Nita Saini

Foreword by Barefoot Doctor

Jayra (UK) Ltd
Moore Stephens
The French Quarter
114 High Street
Southampton
SO14 2AA

First published in Great Britain in 2012 by Jayra (UK) ltd
Copyright c 2012 Nita Saini

Printed and bound in the UK by DEK Graphics.

Dedicated to

Nikhila and Alisha

Your contribution has been far greater
than you will ever know.

Thank you

A massive heartfelt thank you to Steve Wichett of nlpchangeworks.com who changed and improved my life at a time when I most needed it, and of course to Akcelina Cvijectic of akcelina.com who helped me to improve my physical and emotional wellbeing; I truly don't know what I'd have done without you. You are both world class people and agents of change.

To my daughter Nikhila: your contributions to early drafts of the manuscript were substantial and of course to Alisha, for all of your support.

To Dan Delaney, Sam Booth, Lyndsey Booth and Geoff Rolls. Thank you so much for your support, comments and invaluable feedback. To Sandie Murdoch for typing up the script and your valuable feedback – Thank you.

A massive thank you to my editor, Marsha Rickard, for all your support and contribution.

To Akcelina Cjvijetic, Anne Jirsh of annejirsh.com and David Wilkinson for encouraging and supporting me to continue to follow my dream – Thank you.

To Marianne Williamson, for your unwavering permission to allow me to print Our Deepest Fear – Thank you.

And of course to Barefoot Doctor of barefootdoctorglobal.com. Your belief in me and this book massively encouraged and supported me. You spurred me on – deepest, heartfelt gratitude always.

Contents

Moving On Up

Foreword
by Barefoot Doctor

Nita Saini, is a brilliant woman, not just because she's written this exceptional little book, but in the literal sense of shining bright.

She's been to the depths and come back with this jewel. There are many out there peddling remedies for depression in all its guises, but most of it's snake oil and stumbling across the genuine article is rare.

Both this book and its author are the genuine article and I'm proud to trumpet it here. I believe you'll derive enormous benefit from reading it, not just from the marvellously and eloquently presented content but because you'll actually feel Nita's wonderful, fresh, pure, exuberant energy being transmitted through the words and even through the spaces between them – perhaps especially in the latter, as what you're getting here is one of those rare offerings touched by the grace of the divine.

And don't for a moment think that just because it's small in size, it's small in stature. This work has more to say in its little finger, so to speak, than tomes 18 times longer.

I'm happy you have this book in your hands, happy for the benefits it will bring you, and happy we have the privilege of being on the planet together at this time with such a fine person as she.

Barefoot Doctor
barefootdoctorglobal.com

Nita's Offering

It hasn't been easy writing this book

In fact there have been many challenges to overcome. However, for the past six years, following my own journey to happiness, I've had this compelling urge to help others through a book

Here it is. This is my offering.

Nita.

Moving On Up

Introduction

On the surface it was a simple question.

"What do you want? What do you really, really want?"

I couldn't answer the question. It was as if I had been trapped in the depths of darkness for so long. I didn't know my way out.

There is a way out. This pocketbook is your guide. I have been there, I have done it. I know that with the right help, every man and woman of any age can become happier in life.

This book is for anyone who wants to stop feeling down. It is for anyone who wants to be more upbeat. If you are feeling adverse or unhelpful thoughts such as worry, guilt or depression, this book will help. In fact if you are feeling generally happy with life, this book will help further enhance it.

Back then, recurring downbeat thoughts and habits made it extremely difficult for me to even contemplate an upbeat attitude to life. And I came to realise that that's precisely what they were; just thoughts and habits.

Thoughts and habits can be changed. With the invaluable help from a variety of experts, together with what I learnt from my personal development training, I came to realise that my thoughts, habits and behaviours were holding me back. I had become an expert at making myself miserable and believed that no one else in the world could be feeling as bad I was. I now know that I wasn't alone.

After a few years of counselling and therapy, I so wanted to be happier, but I still didn't quite know where to start. One of two major turning points for me (and for just about everybody else I know who has mastered the skills for leading a more upbeat life) was reaching the fundamental decision to make becoming upbeat a life priority. Every day. My burning desire to be more upbeat drove me to break free from the dull, lifeless, downbeat existence that I had been living.

Discovering precisely what to do on a daily basis to achieve this was the second turning point – the missing link.

To give you an idea of timescales, I suffered with depression for seven years. For four of those years I was on high doses of anti-depressants. By practising the techniques in this book and under full medical supervision, it took five months to wean myself off the prescribed medication completely. During this time I eliminated or massively reduced unhelpful thought patterns and habits that had been ingrained for the past

40 years. I've not looked back since 2005. It is important to appreciate that each one of us is unique, timescales for one person may not be the same as for another. There is no right or wrong. Respect your uniqueness and work at a pace that is right for you.

For many years I didn't even like myself. I felt as if I was a terrible person and that I couldn't get anything right. I was consumed with feelings of hopelessness, anger, guilt and even hatred towards myself and others. I had failed to take responsibility for the way I felt. I was proud of being one of life's victims. Bad things happened to me. Nothing was my fault. I was not in charge of my own thoughts and emotions. I was yet to learn that I was the only one who had the power to change them.

As I began changing, I noticed I then progressively, quickly and easily started to become more upbeat.

Included in this pocketbook are the practical techniques and tips that worked in my own recovery.

I remember having far too many thoughts spinning around in my head. I came to realise that this is a common trait amongst downbeat people. To break this cycle, I started doing different things.

So the 'Up Foundations' and the 'Upbeat Reminders' in Chapters One and Two of this pocketbook have been designed to help you with simple activities you can do to instantly feel better. Once these form the foundation of your new life, the journey towards being more upbeat becomes easier and easier.

Chapter Three examines the emotions which most influence how upbeat or downbeat we feel, and includes a method for measuring these emotions using what I call 'The Mood Tracker'. The Recovery Cycle in Chapter Four examines why time can be a great healer and how you can help yourself. The following chapters offer additional practical tips on how you can increase how good you feel about yourself and life in general, and how to break free from the Demons that can contribute to any downbeat moods. A poem by Marianne Williamson has been included to remind you how special you are.

Your beliefs, how you talk to yourself, the pictures you create in your mind and whether you live "in the Now" are contributing factors to how you feel about yourself. They can all be improved to make you feel even happier. These are covered in Chapter Six. Chapter Seven of the book takes each emotion that influences our moods and offers practical ways to minimise or eliminate the negative effects the downbeat emotions can have on our life. The first seven chapters will support you in achieving inner balance and happiness. Chapter Eight uses The Wheel of Life, a very simple and yet powerful technique to help you achieve outer balance in your life.

In the Quick Reference Guides at the back of the book,

you will find a number of methods for tracking your moods and pages that summarise how you can instantly give yourself an upbeat boost.

For those of you who feel you just need a general uplift, read the whole book straight through and then go back and practise the techniques and strategies that are most relevant to you.

For those of you who are feeling low, the best way to make use of this book, so that it is has the greatest impact, is to read and absorb the information first and then do the techniques up to and including Chapter Three. Once you have done these for a few weeks there will be noticeable improvements to your wellbeing. Then, continue to read, absorb and practise the techniques in the rest of the book. Regularly go back over the chapters to help embed the new techniques and strategies to help you become happier and more upbeat.

When I was retraining my own thoughts and behaviours I would carry bits of paper around in my back pocket or bag to remind me how to do things differently, which is why this book is pocket sized. It has therefore been designed specifically for you to carry with you as your constant and supportive companion for happiness.

Sometimes prescribed medication to facilitate or sustain our recovery is the only way we know. Pharmaceutical drugs are only a small part of our recovery process. Many people, including my own doctor told me this was the case. However, it took quite a while for me to get my head around what I could do for myself safely and responsibly.

So ask yourself "How Up do you want to be?" and "How dedicated are you to being more Upbeat?"

The best news for you is that the Up System is free. Doing these activities costs absolutely nothing and requires no medication or artificial stimulants of any kind. This is not a replacement for professional medical attention, however it can always be used alongside it.

It's worth stopping for a moment to think about what 'upbeat' means to you. How would you know when you feel upbeat? What would you see? And what would you hear? What would your life be like? What difference would it make to your life, now and in the future?

Perhaps you believe you do a lot of the stuff that's in this book already. If that's the case – great! The best proof is that you already feel upbeat most days. If you're not feeling this yet, this book is here to help you now.

There are countless people who are brilliant at talking themselves out of why these techniques and strategies won't work for them, believing that they are not appropriate to their situation or needs. They would prefer to remain downbeat than to even consider embarking on simple practices that would help them feel happier. They would prefer to be 'right' than happy. And they stay in that downward spiral.

So if you are prepared to JFDI (Just Flippin' Do It), use as many of the simple, practical ideas in this pocketbook to instantly and permanently become more upbeat. Selecting one or two will have a positive effect, and adopting most of them will help you make massive improvements – quickly.

People with a downbeat attitude to life have developed those habits over time. They become extremely good at thinking themselves into being downbeat: I certainly did. I believed that the world was a harsh place, people couldn't be trusted, so I lived in a state of constant fear and paranoia. Back then, my mind was my biggest enemy.

No matter how young or old you are, can you identify with this form of thinking? If so, just apply the energy you used to give to the downbeat thoughts and habits to the upbeat ones now. This will train your mind to be your best friend. When new upbeat habits have been given a chance to replace and embed themselves into our daily lives, the benefits can be truly astounding.

These days, when you set out on any new journey, you have to figure out the best route. Perhaps you'd decide to use a route planner or a satellite navigation system. Whatever method you use, the system needs to know your starting point.

What's your starting point on your journey towards being more upbeat? To help you upscale your life, use the 'Up Scale'.

The Up Scale

How upbeat do you feel right now on a scale of 0 to 10? 10 being the highest.

In 2003 I was at a two or three on a daily basis and on my worst days I wasn't any better than a one. Looking back I know with certainty that this was mainly due to my habitual, unhelpful thinking patterns. My circumstances weren't actually as bad as I had convinced myself that they were. What made it even more difficult to drag myself out of this desperately unhappy period was how much my low self-esteem and lack of confidence prevented me from making the improvements to the parts of my life that I was so unhappy about. I was also constantly thinking about things that I no longer had any control over because they had already happened – a very long time ago.

My daily average on the Up Scale has improved dramatically. And yours can too.

So, initially use The Up Scale every day to remind yourself of where you are, in that moment.

When using the scale becomes a new habit, it helps you move closer to your preferred destination.

- How much do you want to stop feeling downbeat?
- How strong is your desire to become more upbeat?
- How good are you going to feel?
- How good is life going to be for you, once your daily average on The Up Scale has moved up?

Let us begin....

Chapter 1

The UP Foundations

"You don't have to see the whole staircase. Just take the first step." **Martin Luther King.**

It was a very sunny, quiet day in the Jungle. A tribe of monkeys were playing, eating and wandering around on the jungle floor, going about their daily business. The noise level suddenly rose. In the distance, the monkeys could see a congregation of crocodiles making their way towards them. All but one monkey grabbed as many bananas as they could, and rapidly climbed up the nearest tree, chattering loudly. The remaining monkey continued eating his bananas on the ground "Those crocodiles are miles away" he muttered to himself, "I can't be bothered to move up now." A few moments later the thudding sound of the crocodiles' stumpy legs became more intense. Before he knew it, the crocodiles were virtually on top of him. He left his remaining bananas on the ground and hastily climbed the tree, whilst the crocodiles made one last attempt at catching him by snapping at his tail.

Where would the crocodiles need to be for you to decide to Move on UP?

This story has been included to remind us that we can all move on up, well before things could start to snap. And the easiest and most effective way to move up, is by adopting the five Up Foundations.

After years of trial and error, I recognised these five simple, easy-to-adopt ways to feel more upbeat easily and permanently. Adopting these new behaviours and using them all every single day will give you the maximum benefits for the least amount of time and effort.

Some people could easily decide that a couple of them are too insignificant or trivial to help them be more upbeat.

However, these methods work.

They have been proven to make a positive difference. You may have to force yourself to do this at first, to get the ball rolling. Initially, overcoming any inertia may require a bit of effort, but once you get going, things become so much easier.

Adopt all five of these behaviours for at least two weeks and then assess the results for yourself. You will be pleasantly surprised at how much more upbeat you feel. All it requires is for you to add these into your daily routine. Think of them as your Upbeat Foundation. From today.

1. Go for a Walk

Make walking a whole body experience, move your arms too. Just 20 minutes a day, every day, is all it takes. Walk tall. An upright posture is directly linked to your upbeat mood. And look up as you walk. This too has a beneficial effect on how you feel. Not only will your fitness improve, you may find that any unwanted pounds begin to drop off too!

2. Smile More

Smile right now while you are reading these words. How does it change the way you feel in this moment? Do you feel ever so slightly more upbeat? If smiles have been scarce in your life, think about what has made you smile in the past and what would make you smile now? Jot these things down as a reminder so you can refer to the list throughout the day, and smile as you read. In fact, just deliberately smile for no reason now! JFDI.

You can smile anywhere. At any time. On your own. Or in company. Give it a go for just one minute at a time, at least five times a day. Smiling, deliberately or otherwise, has been proven to massage the pituitary gland which releases serotonin, also known as the 'happy hormone'.

3. Get a Good Night's Sleep

Upbeat people tend to have loads of energy, while some downbeat people feel tired for much of the time. It's amazing how many men and women regularly deprive themselves of sleep and are somehow surprised to discover how exhausted they feel. So make sure you have enough sleep. If sleeping has been difficult for you, there are some tips you might find helpful on page 28.

Some downbeat people try to escape from their emotional pain by sleeping too much. As a consequence they may feel sluggish or groggy. Doing the 'Up Foundations' is an antidote to this.

Energy levels rise and fall naturally during the day. A short rest can be the perfect 'pick me up'. A 10 minute power nap may be just what you need. If you are at work, during a break, find somewhere where you can sit quietly for a few minutes. Sitting in your car might do the trick! If you can't power nap, move on to number 4.

4. Breathe Deeply from the Abdomen

Set aside a few minutes a day, three times a day to inhale deeply through your nose for a count of three, and then exhale, through your mouth, all of the air inside your lungs for a count of five. Repeat this inhale/exhale routine ten times.

Each time you breathe out, imagine you are breathing

out any negative thoughts and emotions. And each time you breathe in deeply, imagine you are breathing in calmness, tranquillity and are boosting your upbeat reserves.

5. Drink More Water

Water is the most underrated magic ingredient for a more upbeat life. So many people who claim they want to be more upbeat, say they'd already heard that drinking more water was highly beneficial yet admit they have never got around to doing it.

Between 55-75% of the human body is made up of water. Approximately 75% of the brain is water. We lose water all the time. It needs to be replenished regularly if we are to function at our best. As the brain is the most vital part of the human body, water is initially directed to the brain before it is directed to the other vital organs and finally to the rest of the body. So, if the body is dehydrated, the brain will certainly not be performing at its best. This in turn affects how upbeat or downbeat we feel.

Make water your drink of choice, rather than relying on tea, coffee or alcohol to lift you up.

Caffeine and alcohol also have the effect of dehydrating us, as they have a diuretic effect flushing water out of our bodies before it's had the opportunity to be absorbed.

A lot of these tips are common sense and because they are everyday activities, we tend to forget about them – this is why the Up Foundations have been included at the back of the book as a reminder.

Chapter 2

Upbeat Reminders

The Up Foundations are designed to be your starting point: simple, ways to get moving towards being more upbeat. The next stage of the Up System walks us through other ways we can have more good moods. Easily.

A proportion of people who tend to feel low devote a lot of their time and energy on others, whilst ignoring their own needs. Either they feel they do not have the time, money or energy for themselves, or subconsciously they mistakenly believe that other people are more important. Look after yourself.

Whenever we nurture ourselves, even in small ways, we increase the release of the happy brain chemicals. The more of these chemicals we have, the happier we feel. It is only when we are replenished with upbeat chemicals that we can truly give to others.

So, be kind to yourself. Do things that make you feel good: every day. Make **you** more of a priority. Because you are worth it!

In this chapter you'll find various activities designed to nurture you and increase the production of the natural 'upbeat' chemicals. Doing at least one from each category each day, increases the likelihood of being happy becoming your new default setting.

You may already know some of these tips, yet how many do you actually do? If not why not?

For a long time I hadn't realised that my thoughts and behaviours were blocking my happiness. I needed strategies to change my unsupportive ways. In what ways are you hindering your happiness?

A very common trait among those experiencing downbeat episodes is the tendency to overanalyse and go deeper and deeper inside their heads. The downbeat thoughts pile up and each new thought gets whacked on top of the pile, adding more and more downward pressure. Add them all together and no wonder it can feel so difficult to drag ourselves out from underneath it all. You can. These downbeat thinking patterns often paralyse us into doing nothing. The secret is not thinking too much about it – Just Flippin' Do It.

Initially, you may also have found that you needed to force yourself to do the five 'Up Foundations'. You may find the same with these simple activities at first.

When I first began making these additional techniques part of my daily routine, I experienced varying degrees of inner-resistance and asked myself the following questions

- What will my life be like if I do nothing?

- How much do the longer-term gains outweigh any short-term effort?

So, What Are You Going To Do Today?

Get Physical
Do any physical exercise today in addition to your daily walk. At this stage it doesn't matter how much or how little because this is just part of becoming more active.

- Go for a bike ride.
- Jog for just 1, 5, 10 or 15 minutes.
- Go to the gym
- Swim.
- Take a dog for a walk (borrow one if necessary).
- Walk up a few flights of stairs instead of taking the lift.
- Step up and down on the bottom step at home for 5 minutes, great for cardio too.

Then congratulate yourself for whatever you did. Remember any physical activity increases our good mood chemicals.

Random Acts of Nurture
- Watch something that makes you laugh out loud.
- Listen to, or play music you find uplifting.
- Get out into nature either on your own or with a friend. Go to a favourite spot perhaps by a river, the sea or in open green areas or even your own back garden or local park.
- If you enjoy it, do some gardening or pick a bunch of flowers and put them in a vase.
- Read an uplifting book or magazine.
- Spend time with a pet or go to a pet shop.
- Spend time with supportive friends and family members
- Dance as if no-one is watching.

Life's Little Indulgences
Whether you are male or female, indulge yourself in healthy ways. For Example:
- Have a long, soothing bath. Use your favourite soaps, shampoos, or candles. Burn essential oils if they help make the experience more pleasurable.
- Have a massage. Pay a professional or ask your partner. Offer to do the same for them.
- Who are the friends who make you feel good about yourself that you haven't spoken with for a while? Call them. Catch up.

Good Mood Foods
- Choose to eat and drink foods which nurture you from the inside out. Certain foods increase the production of serotonin and dopamine, the feel-good hormones. These foods include brown rice, chicken, turkey, eggs, green leafy vegetables, lentils, nuts (especially almonds and peanuts), mackerel, salmon, sardines, tuna, cottage cheese, watermelon, bananas and milk. Eating these foods will also help you sleep more soundly.
- Sometimes if we feel down, we resort to eating 'comfort foods'. Short-term we think they work. Longer-term, they don't. Reduce or eliminate highly processed foods and drinks which reduce the production of the feel-good chemicals and adversely affect our sleep.

Sleep Routine
Getting the right amount of sleep is one of the five 'Up Foundations'. No one can function at their best if they are constantly feeling exhausted. If, in the past you have had problems sleeping, the following may help you:
- If you find yourself thinking of sleep at any time during the day, remind yourself of how well you're going to sleep that night.
- Avoid watching TV or using a computer at least two

hours before bedtime. This helps to quieten the mind in readiness for a good night's sleep.

- Finish eating at least 3 hours before you go to bed, else you will be trying to sleep whilst your digestive system is still awake!
- Create a new night-time routine. When you find one that works, follow it each night.
- Don't read in bed. It stimulates the mind.
- Recurring thoughts and problems that may spin around inside your head can sometimes make sleep difficult. Make up a worry postponement sheet – write any worries on a piece of paper before you get into bed. See Page 91
- In fact, as part of The Up System, only use your bed for sleep and sex!
- For some, but not all, taking a relaxing bath before bedtime relaxes their body. The more our body is relaxed, the more the mind relaxes ready for a good night's sleep.
- Speak gently to yourself when you are in bed, as if you are speaking to a young child that you deeply care for.
- Imagine each muscle in your body softening and sinking into your mattress.
- As you lie there, become more aware of your breathing. Feel your body enjoy relaxing deeper

and deeper.
- As you lie in bed thing of ALL of the things that you are grateful for, fall asleep with these thoughts on your mind.
- Listen to a relaxing CD before going to bed, or while you are in bed.

Gratitude and Appreciation

When a downbeat person sees a beautifully tendered garden, they're more likely to see the weeds. Appreciating the beauty and softness of the flowers, their vibrant colours, and their aroma fades into the background. What do you notice, the weeds or the beauty?

- Developing an 'Attitude of Gratitude' is an incredibly powerful and effective way to lift one's spirits long-term. Some people initially struggle thinking of anything they can be grateful for. They've convinced themselves that life is so difficult, and there's nothing worth appreciating. Make your own list of what you are grateful for. Include who and what you appreciate. This could be your friends, neighbours, relatives, your health, your senses, the warmth of your bed or home, the clothes you wear, a hug with a special person. You can also draw from special moments from your past. Add new things as you experience them. Once you've written them down, read the list often. Daily is best, and for each item, really feel the appreciation and gratitude. In your list you can also include things like compliments and kindness that you receive from others.

To jump-start your thinking visit movingonupnitasaini.com for a comprehensive list of things we can all be grateful for, or refer to the list on page 107.

- There's a game I play that I call the gratitude game which is another sure way to get the gratitude juices flowing. It's easy and fun. This is how it goes...

  Whatever you see around you, say 'Thank you' and feel this sincerely. From seeing the toothbrush that helps to keep your teeth healthy, to the cooker that helps to cook your nutritious meals. You can incorporate anything and everything when you play this game, inside and outside your home. When you are out you will notice, once you begin to be more aware of them, many objects that you can be grateful for. *For example*: the post box and the postal system that allows you to keep in touch with your family and friends across the world. Have you ever considered being grateful to the person who invented it?

We can all learn to play more games of gratitude. What do you see around you, in the people, places and objects? What can you find to be grateful for now, that you've perhaps previously taken for granted?

- Keep a gratitude box. A special box with keepsakes. These could be special photos, a ticket to a memorable event, a note from a loved one, something your child made for you at school.

You may notice that being more grateful for what you already have also brings more good experiences into your life. Dedicating even a minute each day to give thanks, will move us on up, the Up Scale.

Looking Forward to Your Future

Have you ever been too busy to look forward to a special occasion? A fast-paced life can deprive us of these opportunities for joy. Our thoughts feed our future, so look forward to more events and situations (without ignoring the Now) Dream about the future you desire in exquisite, mouth-watering detail, making it a full sensory experience.

By looking forward to your future you will experience good things more than once. Once when you look forward to them, and again when you experience them for real. Our sub-conscious mind doesn't know the difference between a real event and an imaginary one, so anticipating how well things are going to turn out and optimism for future fun events, helps increase the happy chemicals even more. For tomorrow's passion can drive the present.

However, it's only in the Now that you can take action to influence a happier future.

The simple exercises so far in this chapter will help anyone who wants to keep Moving on Up. And can be especially helpful for anyone of any age experiencing challenging life experiences.

Visit movingonupnitasaini.com for a downloadable journal to fill in on a daily basis.

A copy is also included in the summary at the back of the book, on page 109 for you to photocopy. This can be for your eyes only, so you can keep track of how these new ideas are influencing and improving how you feel.

Chapter 3

The Mood Tracker

A mood is a snapshot of how we feel in a particular moment. Our mood right now is the result of a concoction of emotions, for example: fear and worry, with perhaps some happiness. This emotional mix and the weight we attach to each emotion influences how upbeat we feel. Consumed by our busy lives most of us aren't even aware of how we feel from one moment to the next.

We may even rush around on purpose, so we don't have to face how we truly feel. In the hope that if we don't have to face it, it will disappear forever. Unfortunately, painful emotions have a habit of appearing when we least expect them to.

By becoming more aware of which emotions influence you each day and recognising the importance you attach to each one, you will gain a better understanding of how the combination of your emotions contribute to your current sense of wellbeing.

Using the techniques in this book you will learn to minimise their negative effect and therefore make it much easier to nudge yourself up The Up Scale. So stop for a moment every now and then throughout your day and ask yourself:

- What is my mood right now?
- What emotions could be influencing this mood?

People who feel down much of the time, tend to be slaves to their emotions, whereas upbeat people tend to be more in charge of themselves and their emotions.

Below is a list of the most common emotions that influence our moods. Positive emotions are far, far more powerful than any of the negative ones. So even if you've felt a negative emotion for a long time, experiencing even short bursts of positive emotions each day will very quickly counteract the effects of any negative ones. You'll also find that the more doses of feel-good moods you experience, the easier it becomes to have more and more of them. Instead of regretting your low moods, remind yourself to celebrate each good mood period.

Mood Influencers

- Love
- Appreciation and Gratitude
- Happiness and Joy
- Enthusiasm
- Disappointment
- Envy
- Worry or Anxiety

- Anger, feeling annoyed and irritated
- Blame
- Hatred
- Guilt
- Feeling Overwhelmed or Stressed
- Feeling Controlled by others
- Fear
- Loneliness
- Helplessness/Hopelessness

Which of the unhelpful emotions have you attached too much importance to?

The Mood Tracker Table on the next page can help you. Make numerous copies. Alternatively, download a larger version from Movingonupnitasaini.com where you will also see examples of how it might look. Draw an arrow up to the number that represents how you feel at that point in time. 10 being the highest and 0 the lowest.

Over time, by completing this table on a daily basis you may start to see a pattern emerging, revealing which of these emotions have the most effect on your daily moods: the upbeat and the downbeat ones. You can refer to Chapter Seven to help you minimise the impact of any downbeat emotions.

When I was down all those years ago, I experienced enormous difficulty taking charge of my emotions

Moving On Up

because I just didn't have any physical or emotional energy. Everything was too much effort. I kept thinking, "What is the point of anything?".

The Mood Tracker

Date:	0	5	10
Love			
Appreciation and Gratitude			
Happiness and Joy			
Enthusiasm			
Disappointment			
Envy			
Worry or Anxiety			
Anger, feeling Annoyed or Irritated			
Blame			
Hatred			
Guilt			
Feeling overwhelmed or stressed			
Feeling controlled by others			
Fear			
Lonliness			
Helplessness or Hopelessness			

I wanted to be the best that I could possibly be for the sake of my children. So, eventually I took the decision to take responsibility for my own recovery and refused to allow my negative emotions to continue to run my life into the ground. I learnt that we, as human beings, are far more powerful than that. We don't have to be slaves to our downbeat moods. We can all choose to be in command of them.

When we feel good about life, our bodies are flooded with natural 'feel-good' chemicals: serotonin, dopamine and endorphins. Normal levels of serotonin keep us happy and we are more likely to sleep well. Dopamine motivates us. And endorphins are natural painkillers which relieve tension and anxiety. Endorphins are released when we exercise. They give us a natural feeling of euphoria. All the emotions at the top end of The Mood Tracker increase these feel-good chemicals. Conversely, if we experience emotions towards the bottom end of the chart, they drastically deplete the serotonin, dopamine and endorphin levels.

So in order to become upbeat, it is important to do more things that help produce these natural 'Up' chemicals, which in turn contribute to our well-being and make us feel happier. Certain foods also help to increase serotonin and dopamine levels too. See 'Good Mood Foods' on page 28.

We all have the power to move 'up' (or down) this list. Even if you only accomplish ten more minutes a day to feeling uplifted, celebrate what you have achieved. The more you do this, the easier it becomes.

Chapter 4

The Recovery Cycle

"Pain is inevitable as part of the healing process – suffering is optional." **Unknown author**

The way each of us responds to a significant emotional event (for example: bereavement, divorce, redundancy, moving house or country, or a major illness) is unique to us. The emotions we feel, and the length of time it takes for us to – not to forget the event – but to be able to move forward after the event, varies from person to person.

Losing a loved one is undoubtedly one of the most traumatic ordeals we could ever go through and can be one of the most difficult to come to terms with. With a bad relationship we want to let go of it. With a bereavement of someone close to us, it's almost as if we want to hold onto the person and memories of them in an attempt to keep them alive. We might feel that we owe it to that person to keep them alive by recalling memories about them. Whatever happens you will always have special memories of them. They are yours to keep. Ask yourself, How would they want you to continue living your life? What would they like you to do, be or have?

Whether we have been upbeat or downbeat people in the past, each of us would have experienced some lament at the loss of someone or something that is precious to us. This is natural.

There is evidence to show that we experience certain phases before we are able to accept that the event occurred. These phases constitute what is known as the recovery cycle.

Research shows that these phases are not necessarily sequential or equal in length of time and some people may miss one or more of them. Generally these phases are:

- **Shock**. A bombshell when first hearing about the event.
- **Denial phase**. Initial disbelief. "This isn't really happening". "It's just a horrible dream." "This shouldn't have happened." "It's not fair."
- **Realisation phase.** This is realisation that the event did in fact occur. The initial response could be one of anger, guilt or even blame. Blame towards ourselves, towards other people or the world in general.
- **Despair phase.** A sense of loss, desolation, a deep concern over what happens now. "Why me?" "What have I done to deserve this?" "There is no way out." "I can't help myself and neither can anyone else." "I don't want to go on." "My world has just turned

upside down." "How do I go on?"

The despair phase is normally followed by escapism or acceptance of the situation or a mixture of the two.

- **Escapism phase.** By escaping, we do our utmost to hide from the reality of the situation. We could attempt to completely escape by ignoring the fact that the event happened at all. We may, without intending it, make ourselves ill, therefore allowing ourselves to temporarily flee from the situation or we may just physically hide - not venturing out from the safety of our homes.

- **Acceptance phase.** "I accept the fact that life won't be the same again, but it will have to go on." How long someone takes to get to this place varies from person to person. When you accept that the event occurred, you will notice that your confidence and resilience levels increase.

Research shows that the length of time we spend in the dips of despair is inversely proportional to how self-confident and how resilient we are. That is, the more self-confidence and resilience we have the shorter the length of time we spend in the dips. We can all improve our self-confidence and resilience. The techniques in this book can help you.

Have you ever heard the saying 'Time is a great healer?' The graph shows why this is the case. When we have an understanding of what is going on, we are better equipped to do something about it.

There are things you can do to support yourself:

- Allow yourself to accept, honour and express your feelings. You have every right to feel the way you do.
- Be kind and gentle with yourself. Look at Chapter 2 'Upbeat Reminders' for ways you can be more compassionate towards yourself. Practise techniques outlined there.
- Find someone caring to speak with.
- When you are ready, accept that the situation has occurred. This can be much easier for situations that don't relate to a bereavement or a major illness.
- For some losses e.g. a job loss, plan an approach to change the situation, if you want to. Action that plan.

We are all affected by forces that hold us in place in our lives. Forces such as our self-beliefs, self-confidence, social or ethnic pressures. If these forces are depression, downbeat thoughts or feelings, we could get trapped in a depressed state of mind. If we allow these thoughts and feelings to take control of us we could become stuck. It takes a new force, to push us from that point of stagnation to where we allow change and growth.

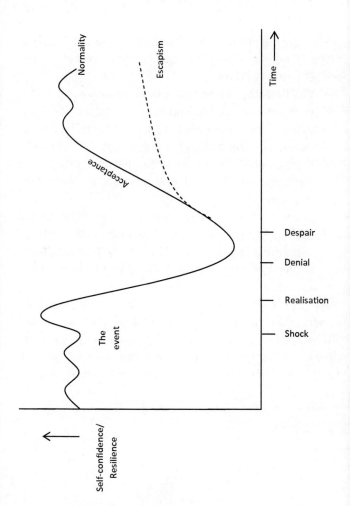

Time →

Normality

Escapism

Acceptance

Despair

Denial

Realisation

Shock

The event

Self-confidence/
Resilience

You can decide to move back up to the crest of the wave. Find something that can be that new force that moves you on and up.

- The first step is having the desire and making that decision to move back up towards the crest of the wave. Time is the greatest healer. Know that as you experience the phases there is a light at the end of the tunnel. With time and the tried and tested techniques in this book both pain and suffering can be eased.
- Secondly, become aware that there are other paths available to you. This awareness could come from something in you; it could be from a therapist, a caring friend or relative. It could be this book.

As you look back, you will notice how all the experiences that you have had, have shaped you to be the wonderful person that you are today. And with your new knowledge, habits and beliefs you can look forward to your new life and becoming the best version of you.

Our Deepest Fear

"Our deepest fear is not that we are inadequate. Our deepest fear is that we are powerful beyond measure. It is our light, not our darkness that most frightens us. We ask ourselves, Who am I to be brilliant, gorgeous, talented, fabulous? Actually, who are you not to be? You are a child of God. Your playing small does not serve the world. There is nothing enlightened about shrinking so that other people won't feel insecure around you. We are all meant to shine, as children do. We were born to make manifest the glory of God that is within us. It's not just in some of us; it's in everyone. And as we let our own light shine, we unconsciously give other people permission to do the same. As we are liberated from our own fear, our presence automatically liberates others."

Chapter 5

Downbeat Demon Crushers

"We don't try to be 100% better rather, 1% better a hundred times." **Anne Mitchell**

We all experience setbacks at times – Demons that hold us back from feeling upbeat - if we allow them to. The Up System recognises this and includes a number of strategies to crush these Demons. This is an essential part of becoming a long-term upbeat person and learning how to spot them is the first step.

People can become addicted to negative emotions if they get caught up in a cycle of feeling a certain way, such as worrying. It's a habit. The mind and body were familiar with this way of thinking even if it's not in our best interest. To get out of the cycle we need to **do** something different. The biggest Demons are the various 'benefits' we perceive in our minds to staying downbeat. For example, if someone is really unwell, they may receive sympathy and attention. So in a perverse way there is a benefit to remaining ill. This might sound really odd – but can you identify with any of the following?

It Feels Easier Not to Bother

Breaking out of this cycle is at the heart of this for some. I know this one very well. There were days when I couldn't be bothered to do anything. Or felt I didn't have the physical strength to even go for a five minute walk. I felt exhausted and a deep numbness. The way out is to do something.

This is how I crushed this Demon. First, I created a mental picture of what my life would be like if I didn't change anything at all. I made this picture big. I saw myself doing the same old stuff – nothing had changed. The feelings and sounds associated with this picture weren't good either. I certainly didn't like the look of that bleak, empty future. I also asked myself who or what would be affected if I remained the way I was, or worse still, if I wasn't around? This definitely motivated me to do things differently. I then made mental pictures of how I wanted to feel and my desired end goal. I made mental images of what I would see, what I'd hear and how I'd feel when doing the Up Foundations. Then I made that picture in my mind bigger, more colourful and more appealing. This empowered me into crushing this Demon. What else would you be able to do when you're happier that you don't do yet?

Ask for support from a family member or a good friend, if you can. Tell them what you are doing and ask them to help you carry out the techniques in this pocketbook regularly.

Alternatively, do one tip from this book each day, however small it appears. Continue with this one technique and add a second technique after say, a week. Remember: do something. Then as the days and weeks go by, look back and notice how much more upbeat you are now compared to just a short while ago.

Believing There's No Other Way

At one point, I was at the end of my tether. I had tried so many different therapies. Initially, this included counselling which focused on the 'problems' in my life. And that stopped me moving forward. I was constantly being asked the question "Why?" Eventually, I came to realise it really didn't matter why something had happened. A far more important question was, "How could I become more upbeat?" "How could I make life happier for me?" Focus more of your time and energy on solutions. If you find seeing a counsellor helpful, ensure that they are solution rather than problem focused.

Taking Things Too Personally

People who feel extremely downbeat often share a sense of feeling completely overwhelmed by what would otherwise be thought of as the most trivial situations. The slightest episode can set-off a downward spiral of emotions.

If we feel fragile, it doesn't take much for us to get upset. Attaching too much importance to relatively minor comments or events can be so easy.

Accept that sometimes bad things happen. Even to good people. It's part of normal life.

Upbeat people take life's challenges in their stride. They have the internal resources to put challenges back into perspective. They maintain the bigger picture. Downbeat people tend to feel that everything is about them. "Why did they say that?" or "Why did they do that?" are common general questions. They feel their pain so intensely. What happens isn't a reflection on them, even if it feels as though it was.

To help yourself feel less involved, carry out this simple technique.

Instead of replaying an upsetting scenario in your mind, imagine playing it onto a cinema screen in front of you whilst sitting at the very back of the cinema so that you see the back of your head and can watch yourself, watching yourself on the screen. On the screen you see the scene including the people who were involved. Watch yourself on the screen. You hear the voices and sounds. Now, change the film from a multi-coloured screening to an old crackly black and white cine film. You can hardly make out what the people are saying. It's just too crackly and the picture is just too fuzzy. Make the screen smaller and smaller until it is small enough to fit on to the surface of a small frisbee. Throw this frisbee into outer space and watch it disappear. Now create a scene of something that lights you up with happiness every time you think about it.

The more often you carry out this simple exercise, either for the same scenario, or different scenarios, the less involved you are, the more calm and detached you become.

Notice how detached and calm you feel now.

Believing They 'Deserve' To Be Downbeat

Some people think they deserve an unhappy life and are unworthy of the good that life has to offer. Years of being told you are unworthy does not mean that it is true. No matter who told you. People who behave in a cruel way, (many of whom would claim that they were actually being kind) often have major 'issues' themselves which they pass on, like an infection to anyone who will listen. It can be extremely difficult to ignore taunts, threats and put-downs, especially from people we love or respect.

Whatever happened in our past, accept it now. 'Accepting' it doesn't mean that it didn't happen or you need to forget about it, it just means that you decide to stop fighting it. This acceptance in itself can offer massive relief.

Acknowledge that you deserve a fulfilling life. That you are worthy of wondrous things happening. Be gentle with yourself. Nurture yourself and know and accept that all marvellous experiences are there for you.

Perfectionism

Nothing is ever good enough for a perfectionist. Being perfect can only ever be a fantasy. For a perfectionist accepting this can initially be too much to bear.

Trying to be perfect can also be a form of protection. Perfectionists sometimes believe that if they get everything just right, they won't have to take painful criticism from anyone else.

Living or working with a perfectionist can be extremely difficult and demanding. But it's nothing compared to the pressures a perfectionist puts on themselves. In fact, when we make mistakes, as we all do, other people warm to us. In a way, it gives others permission to also be 'imperfect'. By being less harsh on ourselves we will find that we are less harsh and expectant of others.

Being 'imperfect' doesn't mean we don't do our best; it means we don't berate ourselves if things don't go according to plan.

Here's how to deal with this Demon:-

- Say 'oh dear, dear, dear, dear, dear ' in a child like manner, in a high pitched silly voice.
- Use the 'mistake' as a fantastic learning experience. What could you chose to do differently if you knew what you know now?
- Accept yourself and the 'mistake' if and when you make 'mistakes'.
- Focus on what you did right.

No human being is perfect. And that's OK.

Sympathy and Attention

Colleagues, family members and friends may offer you loads of sympathy and attention if you're feeling down. That feels good because it's proof that someone cares about you. Sub-consciously we might even convince ourselves that it's worth staying down! When the sympathy and attention stops, as it probably would, where would that leave you? Feeling worse.

Recognise this pattern of thinking. Practise more of what you can do to empower yourself so that you are no longer so reliant on others for your good feelings. Choose the most appropriate techniques from Moving on Up to allow yourself to regain control of your emotions. This will be longer lasting and self-sustaining. Ask friends and family to support you in far healthier ways. This then gives you back your power.

R.A.P.I.D. Demon Crusher

To crush any Downbeat Demons, you can also follow the five step approach below:

- **Recognise** which Downbeat Demon you are experiencing.
- **Accept** that you feel like this. Say to yourself 'Yes I do feel .... and that's OK'.
- **Protection**. Remember that all Downbeat Demons have a positive intention. It doesn't matter if you do not know what it is, but consider what this Downbeat Demon was protecting you from.
- **If** you chose to hold onto these Demons, what is this costing you, not only in how you feel but in other areas of our life?
- **Do** something about becoming more upbeat. Read and do the strategies in Moving on Up.

You can also do the following simple exercise if a demon tries to infiltrate. Once you've carried out the following exercise a couple of times, you will be able to do it any time, any place and anywhere instantly. You have what it takes to crush these Demons.

For example: If it felt easier not to bother, just focus

on that feeling and notice where that appears in your body. Imagine there are taps in your fingers and toes. Imagine this unsupportive feeling flowing with ease out through these taps into the centre of the Earth. Keep these taps open until your mind and body are free from this unsupportive feeling. Breathing steadily and deeply all the time. You know you have the power within you to turn this around to something far more supportive. Imagine a white light surrounding you now, imagine this comforting, powerful light washing over you. Decide on an empowering emotion or skill that you want and fill each and every cell of your mind and body with **its** depth and power. Allow your mind and body to be completely bathed in this new empowering emotion. Savour, delight and indulge yourself in this feeling as its warmth envelops and caresses you. Luxuriate and delight in this. Once you have this feeling, press your thumb and index finger together on either hand. Keep pressing it together. Let it go after about 30 seconds.

Whenever you wish, you can revisit these feelings of support, strength and power. Just press your thumb and index finger together. You can do it now. Anywhere and any time.

Chapter 6

B.E.I.N.G

As well as emotions which influence our moods, these factors also contribute to how we feel about ourselves:

- **B** Our **B**eliefs
- **E** Our self –**E**steem: how good we feel about ourselves
- **I** **I**nternal conversations and internal pictures
- **N** Living in the **N**ow
- **G** **G**oals

Let's take each of these factors in turn and demonstrate how you can improve your moods by adopting these strategies.

BEING – **Beliefs**

Baby circus elephants have a rope tied to their back leg. This rope is wrapped around a heavy stake in the ground. The young elephant is not strong enough to break free. Over time the older and much stronger elephant learns to not even try to escape. It has now convinced itself that it cannot break free. The trainer can then tie a loose rope around the mature elephant's leg, attached to a small, weak stake. Many of us grow up to be like these elephants.

Because of earlier life experiences, when we were much younger and vulnerable, we have beliefs imposed upon us, that in our adult life hold us back from reaching our full potential.

- What beliefs do you have about yourself that you or others planted in your mind, years or even decades ago?
- How would you behave knowing that you have an enormous amount of inner strength and unlimited positive qualities?
- What would you say and do differently?

If you think that you are not capable of improving yourself, or your situation, that is a belief in itself. They are recurring thought patterns that you've learned to give more attention to than they deserve. Which beliefs is it time to untie yourself from?

The more we believe in ourselves and the world in general, the more UP we feel. What beliefs do you have?

- What do you believe about the world?
- Do you believe that people are out to get you or that people do their best and want to help you?
- Do you believe that it is not possible to change?
- Or do you believe that, through some action on your part, you can change and change is easy and fun.

Do you do any of the following?
- Tell yourself that things are going to work out badly as they have always done?
- Focus on how bad life is and how it's never going to improve?
- Do you tell yourself (or do others tell you) something with such force and certainty that you just accept it is as 'fact'? Under closer scrutiny, most are merely opinions dressed up to look like facts. We sometimes too readily accept what we've said or heard as being true.

It's often the same with beliefs. Which ones are merely opinions and not facts?

If there are any beliefs that no longer serve you, accept that these beliefs were the best possible beliefs for you at that time. Today, you are much stronger, more experienced and possess more resources to deal with life. You can replace old, outdated beliefs with new alternatives that are far more relevant and helpful now.

Changing Beliefs

Have fun with this seven step therapeutic process. It will help you discard unwanted beliefs and replace them with more empowering ones:

1. Picture in your mind's eye something you believe with great certainty. If you believe the sun will rise tomorrow – picture this.
2. Hold that picture in your mind. See what you see, hear what you hear and feel what you feel. Notice where in your body you have the feeling. Hold the feeling it gives you. Notice where in your mind the picture is located. For example: is it close, far away, to the left or to the right? Is it front of you or behind? Inside or outside your head?
3. Now think of an old belief that was holding you back? For example: I believe that changing the way I think is difficult. Notice where this picture is. Point to it. You will discover it is not in the same place. Suspend this belief for a moment.
4. Now change it. For example: I believe that making changes to the way I think is easy.
5. Bring to mind the feelings of great certainty associated with the picture you saw in step 1. Remember where it was located.
6. Now say the new desired belief whilst holding the feeling and the location of your picture from step 1.
7. Hold onto this for 15 seconds or so and keep repeating the new belief to yourself.

As beliefs normally come before actions, you will notice

that your actions will support this new belief.

These affirmations will also help you:-
- As each day passes, this becomes easier and easier.
- I deserve a healthy, happy and fulfilling life.
- **BETOP – B**elieve **E**verything **T**urns **O**ut **P**erfectly
- The older I get the healthier, happier and more fulfilled I am.
- I choose to 'Live Magically'. Gill Edwards, livingmagically.com

Say these often: when you are washing up, doing the gardening, in the shower, etc. and say these with feeling, feeling good as you say them, knowing that this will become your new default setting. Write these and other affirmations on cards and stick them up around your home in places where you will see them often. Make a point of pausing to read and absorb them.

To enhance this process further, do this:

Close your eyes and visualise that your future is bright and you can change whatever you want to change because something profound is beginning to happen. Great images of your wonderful future are popping up and making it possible to create the changes you want.

Magnify every great moment you've ever had. Every fibre of your soul and being wants to feel good. Say to yourself, "Life is good." All kinds of things are possible in the Universe. The Universe is a friendly place. Practise daily pushing any bad pictures far away and pulling good pictures closer to you. When you do this, any fear dissolves and you open yourself up to amazing possibilities of great and positive things happening.

BEING – Self-Esteem
"No-one can make you feel inferior, without your consent." **Eleanor Roosevelt**

"It's just not worth it! I'm not worth it!" Those were the words repeated endlessly by my friend, who I will call Jenny. She had been in a relationship with a man for ten years. He would expect all of her time and energy. Yet whenever she asked for anything, he wouldn't be there for her. However much she gave him, it was never enough. I asked her why she put up with this sort of behaviour. She had convinced herself that she wouldn't be able to find anyone better!

Self-esteem is how good you feel about yourself. If we have low self-esteem we feel we are unworthy of so many things: love, happiness, friends, a fantastic relationship, a great rewarding job, a nice home, a dream car, that holiday of a lifetime etc. Jenny didn't feel worthy of a fulfilling relationship. You'll be pleased to hear that Jenny did eventually do what was best for her and leave, and in doing so her self-esteem, and her life, improved enormously. Not surprisingly.

There are a number of reasons why our self-esteem and confidence could have been knocked in the past. However, why something happened is not always a helpful question. A better question to ask, "How can this be improved, even just a little – right now"

First assess how high your self-esteem currently is using this amended version of The Rosenberg Self –Esteem Scale. Answer the following questions by putting a number in each box. Strongly agree = 4, Agree = 3, Disagree = 2, or Strongly Disagree =1. 4 being the highest score, i.e. a healthy self-esteem.

The scale

- I like/love/accept myself. ☐

- I am a good person most of the time. ☐

- I have many good qualities. ☐

- I can achieve the things I want to.

☐

- I have much to be proud of.

☐

- I am of value to myself and others.

☐

- I respect myself.

☐

- All in all, I am inclined to feel that I am a success.

☐

- I have a positive outlook.

☐

Total:

☐

Anything above a score of twenty suggests a healthy self-esteem.

If there are any of the above that you didn't quite believe about yourself yet, say these to yourself often, every day, with sincerity until you realise that you have these qualities.

Here is a collection of instant, practical ways you can improve your self esteem:

- Create a 'self-appreciation board' with your

name in the middle. Add qualities you know you possess, then ask your most trusted friends, family and colleagues what they particularly like and admire about you. Add these qualities to the board. Mount the board onto a wall where you will remember to look at it and read it daily. Offer to contribute to an appreciation board for your family, friends and colleagues.

- Look into your eyes as you look into a mirror and tell yourself how much you like and/or love yourself. Thank yourself for getting yourself to where you are today, and know that All is Well. I know many people who initially had trouble looking at themselves in a mirror (including myself). If you can't yet do this, say it to yourself without the mirror to begin with.

- Remember the times you have felt liked or loved by others. Relive the way they looked at you, how they told you what they felt about you. Remember what friends and family have done to show they care about you. Feel the warmth of their love towards you.

Having a healthy self-esteem allows you to 'just be yourself', be comfortable in your own skin and accept yourself for who you are.

BEING – Internal Conversation

Have you ever started off on a car journey and before going out the door asked yourself "Now, where did I put those keys?" We all talk to ourselves silently. It's quite normal. If a little voice is telling you that you don't – that was it! This inner-voice can make your life a misery or help you. It's your choice.

For example: as a result of not being able to find your keys you set-off on your journey later than planned. You're now sitting in a traffic jam saying to yourself, "I'm going to be late. This is going to be a disaster. They'll never believe me. They'll be so unimpressed that I'm late." How often have you said this to yourself? This is a sure way to keep you feeling stressed about a situation you can do nothing about.

Those who have learned to accept such a situation discover that their whole body relaxes. They find something to enjoy whilst they are stationary: listening to music, admiring the scenery or perhaps having a conversation with passengers in the car.

In a split second you too can become more relaxed whatever situation you are in. Simply choose to accept the reality of the situation. Breathe deeply and chose to live in the moment. Remind yourself to switch your thoughts to whatever is good. And BETOP – Believe Everything Turns Out Perfectly. And do it with a smile.

Some of our negative thoughts are weeds that have taken root over many years. Overgrown and unwanted they may need a little effort to replace them with more helpful, empowering thoughts. You can do this. And quickly. You decide that the time has arrived. Now.

Dr Emoto carried out an experiment to discover how thoughts and spoken word affect us. www.masaru-emoto.net

He took water from a natural water source and filled a number of containers with it. He either said, wrote or thought, different words to the different containers. For example: I love you, you make me sick, I hate you, love and gratitude. He then froze this water and photographed the crystals that were produced. The crystals formed from the water that had had positive words spoken to it or written on it, or thought to it, were far more beautiful and symmetrical than the water with negative words. Conversely crystals did not form at all or were ugly from the negative thoughts and words.

As the human body is made up of 55% - 75% of water, the only conclusion that there can be is that what we say to ourselves will affect how we feel. This also applies to what we think about, or say to other people too.

There have been a number of scientific experiments conducted, with similar results of how our thoughts and words effect us. Dr Candace Pert, a leading scientist, is another pioneer in this field. She wrote two fantastic books 'Molecules of Emotion' and 'Everything You Need to Feel Go(o)d'.

At first, it's quite common to be unsure about whether a thought makes you feel good or bad. If you are ever uncertain, stop for a moment and ask yourself the question: "How does this thought make me feel?" Once you know which thoughts make you feel bad, it gets easier to replace them with more helpful ones. To start with, have a positive thought ready, so that if a negative thought does ever pop into your mind, you can quickly and easily replace it with a positive one. For example: replace any negative thought with the thought of someone you love.

How often do you use words that harm, or words that hug? Notice the actual words that you use when you speak to yourself. How does it make you feel when you use the following words?

I **should** wash the dishes.
I **must** wash the dishes.
I **have** to wash the dishes.

Now notice how you feel when you replace those words with any of the following:

I **want** to wash the dishes.
I **might** wash the dishes.
I **choose** to wash the dishes.

Did you find that by saying the words in the second list it took the pressure of you to wash the dishes? The words in the second list give you choices. They are not unreasonable demands.

By noticing how often you use words that harm you, or hug you, you become far more attuned to how supportive you are to yourself. You'll then be able to increase the frequency of use of those supportive words.

Realise that you can make these changes instantly. Play around with this language in your mind and before you know it, you will be giving yourself more choices, which in turn will help you each and every day to be uplifted.

When I was retraining my own internal conversation, I created a much shorter version of the table on the next page which I carried around in my back pocket. When I caught myself having any of the unhelpful thoughts in the left column, I would refer to the card and use the more helpful alternatives in the right column. There is a copy of this as a download on my website: movingonupnitasaini.com.

Mind Chatter Reminders

I do not feel in control	Remember a time when you felt in control. How did you stand or sit? Get into the same stance now and think back to how you felt when you were in control.
You have two possible options and neither is really appealing.	Ask yourself "What **can** I do?" What am I prepared to do that is acceptable to me.
I will **try** to do that	I **will** do that.
I **can't** do this it's all new	I **can** do this, I've learnt many new things in my life already

I want to do this stuff **but** I don't have time. I want to feel more upbeat **but** I don't know if this will work	Change the order of the sentence so that it ends in the positive. I don't have time **but** I want to do this stuff. I don't know if this will work **but** I want to feel more upbeat.
What if everything turns out badly again. **What if** it doesn't work out. This generates endless negative scenarios.	What if... it works **amazingly** well.
All or nothing. These improvements **all** have to work or else it's not worth doing. It **all** has to work out perfectly. If not, I will be a failure.	This process is gradual. Accept this. Notice what is improving and how this affects your mood.

I am flawed because I can't get **anything** right. For example: I am a lousy parent.	No one is perfect. We all make mistakes. It is part of being human. Mistakes can be a fantastic learning experience. Think about what you have got right in the past, however small those achievements may appear to you.
People sometimes expect a miracle cure I expect to feel ecstatic all the time. And NOW!	Adopt this mindset "If it's to be, its up to me" Accept personal responsibility

However many years a bad thought has been a bad habit, research shows that by persisting with the new thoughts, it takes about a month for new thoughts to become new habits.

BEING – Internal Tone of Voice

It's not just what **we** say to ourselves, but **how** we speak to ourselves that also contributes to how we feel. When you listen to your internal conversation, what is its tone of voice? Is it predominantly harsh, or kind? Soft or loud? Someone who is being supportive of another person sounds very different to someone who is being critical. A critical internal dialogue with a harsh tone will definitely keep you down.

Have a go at this, Say to yourself in a monotone, flat, lifeless voice "I feel great". How did that make you feel?

Now say "I feel great!!" say it with sincerity, vibrancy, positive spirit and with a song in your voice.

Which one made you feel more upbeat? Hopefully, the second one. This shows simply how our tone of voice affects our moods.

Notice more often the tone you use to speak to yourself. By learning to recognise and being more aware of those times when your tone of voice is being critical, you can instantly switch it to the same voice you would use to support your best friend or a young child.

BEING – Internal Cinema

Just imagine you are planning the perfect relaxing beach holiday. The ideal destination. Beautiful scenery. Fantastic weather. Clear blue skies. Beautiful beaches that go on for miles. Perfect evenings.

Now imagine the same holiday but with awful weather: incessant rain, black cloudy skies and high winds. The resort is dirty and overcrowded. You can't do the things you wanted to do.

Which cinema screening of your holiday contributed to making you feel more upbeat? Hopefully, it was the first example.

The pictures that we create in our minds directly influence how we feel. Bad pictures = upsetting feelings. Good pictures = good feelings. We all create pictures in our minds although some people develop ways of focusing more on the good and also making their good pictures brighter, sharper and bigger. You can too.

Researchers asked two teams of basketball players to carry out the following experiment. The first team **visualised** shooting basketballs into the net for a whole week, and the second team **physically** practised shooting basketballs into the net for the week. At the end of the week, they both **physically** shot basketballs on the court. The team that visualised had improved their scores by far more than the team that had practised on the basketball court. It doesn't mean that we **just** need to visualise, it means that when we visualise **and** practise, we can influence our future in great ways.

People like Bill Gates, co-founder of Microsoft, know this. They take time out of their busy day, to visualise not only their day, but their future. They know that their future tomorrow, are the pictures that they created in their mind today. We don't have to be the owners of global corporations to do this. We can all do this.

And if you think that you don't make pictures, ask yourself, what colour is your kitchen? You'll only know the answer by picturing it in your mind – unless you're standing in your kitchen of course!

You can choose which shots you're going to make in your own life 'feel good' movie. Imagine that you are on the cinema screen, with you in the starring role of your own blockbuster movie.

Do you **want** to include elements of your life that are not what you would prefer them to be? Or would you prefer to include a storyline that was more upbeat? Again, it is your decision.

For the purposes of this next exercise you can put to one side what you believe is realistic. Picture this:-

Who do you choose to accompany you? Now? In the next few months? The next year? How much more do you want to see yourself smiling, laughing, and having fun? Where are you living? What does it look like? What are the people saying? What other sounds do you hear? How does it feel living in this place? Where are you working? What experiences are you enjoying?

When you have your preferred pictures in perfect

focus, step into the picture, and fully enjoy and appreciate your life: who and what do you hear and see around you? Relish in how good this all makes you feel. Replay this movie in your mind as often as you wish. By focusing more on these types of moving pictures it will help you move on up, the Up Scale.

BEING – Now

Some people are so engrossed in their future or consumed by their past they aren't able to enjoy what's happening in their present, in the here and now.

Now, you could be having fun with your children, be out with friends, be working, cleaning, studying, playing sport, or even doing nothing – just being.

The easiest way to live in the Now, is to:

- Be mindful, absolutely focused and fully immersed in whatever you're doing.
- Along with this, appreciate the benefits you receive from carrying out the activity. Appreciation in itself will uplift you. Recognising the benefits this will bring will also help you to accomplish things with ease and excellence.

When you do these two things, you will truly be living in the Now.

For example: If you're washing your car, avoid thinking about what you could be doing instead. Completely immerse yourself in washing your car. Appreciate the benefits you will gain by washing it – what do you **get** from washing your car? What are the advantages you perceive?

If you're scrubbing the kitchen floor, don't be thinking about, how after the kids get home it'll be dirty again. Instead think about how nice it is to live in a home that is well cared for. Think about the fact that you're physically capable of cleaning the floor. Think about the fact that you have children and a family to make it dirty. Think about how when you do housework, it makes the house look beautiful for you and your family.

This thought provoking poem is a wonderful reminder that our point of power is in the present moment.

Look well to this Day
For it is Life...
The very Best of Life!
In its brief course lie all
the Realities and Truths of Existence
the Joy of Growth!
the Splendour of Action!
the Glory of Power!

For Yesterday is but a memory
and Tomorrow is only a vision
but Today, if lived well*, makes
every yesterday a Memory of Happiness
and every tomorrow a Vision of Hope
Look well therefore to this day!

* Be and Give* the best you can in all your tasks
and relationships, now.

Ancient Sanskrit Poem

BEING – Goals

Having a goal, something that is important to you, will help you Move on Up.

A goal is an intention with a target date. Promises to yourself that can be enormous (for example: I am going to win an Olympic Gold Medal) or that can be smaller such as drinking water throughout the day. And goals can be short, medium or long-term.

Here's how you can accomplish your goals to help yourself be happier:-

- Focus on the end goal and give it a target date. For example: I want to increase the reading on my Up Scale by least one point over the next two months.
- Define it in writing and in the present tense as if you have already achieved it. For example: I am so grateful now that I am more in charge of my moods.
- Focus on what you want, not what you don't want.
- Immerse yourself in what each goal looks and sounds like. How are you going to feel once you've accomplished that goal? What will your life look, feel and sound like?
- Break the goal down into bite-sized chunks. Do one step at a time, however small it is.
- Every time you achieve a goal, reward yourself in an appropriate way.
- Be thankful for having achieved a goal.

Even if you spend half an hour on a goal each day over a year that equates to 182 hours, approximately 8 days. Therefore, each day you're half an hour closer to realising it.

Chapter 7

The Mood Tracker Menu

In chapter three we identified a range of emotions and how they affect our moods. Here we take each of those in the reverse order they appeared in The Mood Tracker.

The following emotions affect different people in different ways. However, it's the combined negative effects of these emotions that can drag us down. If we allow them to. Therefore, consider each of the emotions that affect you the most and carry out the strategies for overcoming them. Remember to use the Up Foundations and the Upbeat Reminders too.

Feeling helpless or hopeless

Feeling lost or helpless is like being locked in a tiny room without any doors or windows. And with no way out: a state of feeling numb, just existing not living. Underlying beliefs and recurring thought patterns contribute to these feelings. Unsupportive ones can be replaced. They are not facts.

When we do the same things, we always get the same results. To transform our thinking into an upward spiral, DO something different.

- Accept that this is how you feel at the moment. It's

OK. Be kind to yourself.

- Without thinking abut it – just **do** any or all of the Up Foundation.
- If you've been feeling hopeless and helpless in a specific chair or room, sit in a different chair or go to a different room.
- Be with more people who lift you up.

Loneliness

Loneliness can be the beginning of the downward spiral. The more lonely we feel, the more unsociable we might want to be. Recognise this cycle as early as possible. Refuse to allow yourself to think of 'better' times, or why you feel the way you do. Instead turn your focus outwards. Perhaps join a voluntary group or volunteer to help someone in need. This helps them and it helps you to break this loneliness cycle. Commit to getting out more by making appointments with cheerful friends, colleagues and extended family members.

Recognise that 'loneliness' and 'being alone' are different. 'Being alone' is something you choose.

Fear

We are born with only two fears: fear of falling and fear of loud noises. We learn everything else! They can be unlearned.

Fear has been described as **F**alse **E**vidence **A**ppearing **R**eal. When people allow themselves to be consumed by fear it can be a self-fulfilling prophecy. This then re-affirms the justification for the fear "I knew things would turn out badly" Fear has our best interests at heart. It has a positive intention. Sometimes it exists to protect us from physical harm or to reduce potential risk.

Therefore some fear is good: being fearless can be totally irresponsible. Fear only becomes a problem if we allow it to take over our lives.

What have you been fearful about? What is the worst that can happen? If the worst happened would it really make much difference to you in say, twelve months time? If this outcome was significant, what could you actually do to prevent or minimise its impact? Therefore, ask yourself:

- What is my preferred outcome? Put more energy and attention into this preferred outcome. Imagine that this preferred outcome has already happened. What do you see in your mind's eye? What are you saying to yourself now that you have this preferred outcome? How do you now feel?
- What actions do you need to take now to encourage this preferred outcome? Do them.

Feeling Controlled by Others

"If you don't have a plan for yourself – you become part of someone else's" **Anonymous.**

At times parents, teachers, partners, bosses and even friends put us under pressure to do what they want us to do. Have you ever felt controlled by others? It might be easier in the short-term to give into these requests. By doing this we are giving away our power and we shrink just a little. Feeling as if we have no say about these situations can contribute to downbeat feelings. Here is how you can help yourself:

- Learn to recognise much sooner when someone is trying to control you. Smile to yourself for noticing it. Realise that so many people who try to control others have chronic low self-esteem. They believe if they can put others down, they will somehow feel better about themselves. It doesn't work. Their insecurities are something that they need to resolve for themselves, they are not your problem.
- If expressing yourself is difficult, use CAF to help you: To **C**hange the situation, **A**void it, or change the way you **F**eel about it.
- If you can, ask them "What are you trying to achieve by treating me in this way?" Find out their

intentions.

- Learn to be more assertive by expressing your opinions and feelings more often.
- If possible, remove controlling people from your life. If they are family members or senior work colleagues limit your exposure to them.

Feeling Overwhelmed or Stressed

With never ending 'to do' lists, family responsibilities, work deadlines and demands from bosses we can so easily feel overwhelmed. Eager to please, we keep saying "Yes" to everyone and everything. Until one day, we just can't cope. Sound familiar?

Taking on too much, seems to be a 21st century plague. Those who feel overwhelmed often perceive situations as being far, far more important they actually are. They feel as if they are carrying the entire weight of the world on their shoulders. Some are better able to manage these tensions than others. This is what they do:-

- They accept themselves for who they are. Copy this attitude.
- They don't feel the need to be a martyr.
- They step back and look at the bigger picture and prioritise.
- They ask, "What's the worst that can happen if I don't get this done?" and "How important will this be in 12 months time?"

- They have learned how to say "No" politely and assertively to those who make unreasonable requests and demands. Practise saying "No" in a kind way, in front of the mirror if you wish.
- When they have large tasks to complete, they break them down into smaller more manageable bite-sized chunks.
- They enlist help from others and delegate.

Guilt

"Guilt is regret for what we've done or not done."
Anonymous.

Remember that every emotion has a positive intention. Sometimes guilt is there to remind us not to repeat the same mistakes. We all make mistakes. And when we do, it doesn't mean we are bad people. We actually learn from making mistakes.

If it's possible, say "I'm sorry," to those you think you have hurt. If you can't apologise face-to-face, imagine them sitting opposite you and the favourable response or forgiveness you receive from them.

Forgive yourself and others. Whatever happened, happened. Let it go. You are not helping anyone by punishing yourself.

Moving On Up

Sometimes we feel guilty as a result of the morals/beliefs imposed on us by family, friends, communities or peer groups. As a child we may have been told the same things so many times, we no longer even question how relevant, valid or true they were.

- What beliefs have contributed the most to your feelings of guilt?
- Whose beliefs were they? Yours or someone else's?
- Refer to the belief changes on page 59.
- Accept and appreciate that you know so much more than those who tried to impose their self-limiting beliefs on to you.
- What would you prefer to feel instead of guilt?
- Release and let go of any guilt by imagining the guilt to be a liquid. Allow this to flow freely through the imaginary taps in your fingers and toes, shaking it off into the Earth. What would be a far more supportive emotion to replace the guilt? Now imagine this new emotion starting off in the centre of your body and allow this emotion to fill your entire body. Take this new supportive feeling with you throughout the days to come.

Hatred

"Hatred is like drinking poison and expecting the other person to die." **Anonymous**

The person you feel hatred towards probably doesn't even know how you feel. And if they did, they might be delighted! Either way, they still have a strong hold over you. Why punish yourself by continuing to feel this way?

- Accept that you feel this way.
- Imagine the person sitting opposite you. Think of what you would say to them and how you would like them to respond. Imagine the entire scene.
- Feel compassion for the person you hated. Consider how their upbringing contributed to their behaviour. Think of them as a small vulnerable child, perhaps without the love or attention they craved and deserved. We all do the very best we can with the knowledge and experience we have in that particular moment.
- Forgive them. Let it go. This does not mean that you forget what happened. You are not doing this for them, you are doing this for you. It is a gift to yourself. Accept this gift with gratitude.

Imagine what it will feel like when you experience indifference to this person or situation. It is possible even over a very short period. I know.

Blame

When I first heard the saying "if it's to be, it's up to me," it absolutely shook me to the core. By blaming everyone and everything else for all the pain in my life, I had been able to hand-over complete responsibility for everything that went 'wrong'. Once I realised that I was responsible and accountable for what happened in my life, I felt a sense of empowerment, a lightness. Now that I realised that I was responsible for the situations and events in my life, I had the power to change them and it felt great.

As uncomfortable or scary as this may seem initially, each time we blame someone else for anything, we give away our ability to resolve our own difficulties. By blaming others for what is happening we are giving them control of our emotions and our lives. Do you really want to do that? Let go of all blame. Take back your personal power by refusing to allow yourself to blame anyone else. Accept that you have all the internal resources to handle whatever shows up in your life. You really do.

Anger, Feeling Annoyed and Irritated

How often have you lost your temper, shouted or

screamed at someone else? Most of us have done so (and regretted it) at some point. It's normal to feel angry occasionally. It's how we deal with anger that makes a difference. It is better to deal with it in a way that is acceptable to yourself and those around you.

Some people implode rather than explode when they feel angry. Holding onto anger can be counterproductive. When someone internalises these feelings they have a nasty habit of coming out when you least expect them to. It is far better to learn to let out these emotions before they fester and drag you down. Over time they often evolve into bitterness and resentment. Which could make things feel worse.

- We can feel angry when our boundaries are violated. Anger gives us the strength to deal with this. For example: when your children are unrelenting in their demand for your attention, time or money.
- Sometimes we are prone to getting angry when we're tired or stressed.
- Recognise the trigger that makes you feel angry. Either avoid these situations or prepare yourself by:
    - o Taking deep breaths before going into any of these situations.
    - o Imagine it going really well. A win/win situation for both parties.
    - o Be assertive and express your opinions in a

reasonable manner and allow others to do the same.

o Accept yourself for who you are and accept others and their own lack of perfection too.

o If you find that you are getting angry, be assertive and say "I can't talk to you about this right now, but I really want to resolve this".

o If you ever find that you have any pent up anger, release it in an appropriate way. For example:

o Do some physical exercise

o Shout and scream at the top of your voice in a remote place: such as the top of a hill or facing out to sea on a stormy beach.

Worry and Anxiety

"If you're going to make up stuff, make up good stuff."
Richard Bandler.

Worry puts attention in the wrong direction. It is either thinking negatively about things that 'might' happen in the future or thinking negatively about events that happened in the past. It is a habit. That can be changed. Like other outdated, unsupportive habits, you will have to make a concerted effort to change it. However, worry can be debilitating so the long term benefits will far outweigh any short term efforts. Do these simple things to allow yourself to get off the worry wheel, for it achieves nothing and consumes your valuable time and energy.

- Be aware that you were worrying.
- Replace the pictures, sounds and feelings you created about this situation with how you would like things to be instead.
- A lot of the time we worry about things that never happen.
- Some people believe that if they worry enough, it won't ever happen. This is not true. The more we focus on the worrying situation, the more likely it is to happen. We get more of what we focus on.
- Some worry can be positive as long as we take action to counteract the worry. For example: if someone has poor health, they do things to actively improve their health.
- **BETOP** – **B**elieve **E**verything **T**urns **O**ut **P**erfectly. Say this to yourself with unwavering belief.
- If you find you worry before bedtime and it affects your sleep, write down:
    1. "I am worried about ......?"
    2. Put a positive slant on any worry (For example: money worries. "I budget wisely").

3. "I postpone this worry until 9am tomorrow morning"

- Reflect on everything you are grateful for.
- The opposite of worry is to trust – trust that all is well, trust that right now you are just where you are supposed to be, trust that all is well in your world.

Envy

"Envy is the art of counting another fellow's blessings instead of your own." **Harold Coffin**

Envy is the green eyed monster that arises when we judge ourselves against other people and find our own lives lacking by comparison. A happy person doesn't tend to feel envious of others, they are comfortable in their own skin and are content and appreciative for what they have. Accept that feeling envious will never help you feel good about yourself.

- If envy visits you, it's an early warning sign that you are feeling vulnerable or insecure. Recognise this and do something you know makes you feel better about yourself.
- What do you take for granted about your life? Recall everything (not just material possessions) you can think of that you can be thankful for.
- If someone can do, or has something that you want,

you can also delight in their experience as if it were your own. Just step into their shoes. See what they saw and what they heard and felt. It actually feels good to do this. This allows you to have the same feel good chemicals as if the experience were actually your own.

- If you have to carry out any comparisons, compare yourself to who you were a few weeks ago or a year ago and notice and appreciate how far you have moved forward.

Disappointment

Disappointment is another emotion that occurs when reality doesn't match what we want. When we disappoint ourselves or another person lets us down, we rate our or their performance against what we decided we wanted to have happened. Disappointment then follows.

- Mentally shake off any disappointment.
- Accept the reality of the situation.
- In instances where you felt let down by others, be honest with yourself – did you expect someone to read your mind?   Could you have communicated your expectations sooner?
- If you can't change what has happened, you can change the way you feel about it. For example: if

somebody fails to carry out a promise, don't take it personally. Put yourself in their shoes to understand their reasons. This isn't about making excuses for them. Do this to make yourself feel better.

- What have you learnt to do differently in similar situations?
- How much worse could the outcome have been?

Enthusiasm

Enthusiasm is the spark that makes anything possible. To light that spark or allow it to become even brighter, you can:

- Identify what sort of things you are enthusiastic and passionate about and do more of these things.
- Make big colourful pictures in your mind's eye of you doing these activities. What do you hear? How good do you feel? Then JFDI.
- Do more new things to discover hidden passions.
- Allow those enthusiasm endorphins to flood your mind and body.
- What you focus on, you get. So the more you focus on activities that enthuse you, the more of these experiences you will have. Look forward to more of these.

Happiness and Joy

Happiness is like a whole body smile. It's as if each and every cell of our body is grinning from ear to ear!

Happiness expert Robert Holden PhD believes that we simply forget to be happy. We put happiness off for some other time; when we've lost that weight, bought that latest accessory, got that promotion, etc. Millions of people get so wrapped up in their daily to-do's, pursuing achievement and driving themselves towards a happiness mirage that is always on the horizon of their life: it's vaguely visible but constantly out of reach. Happiness is inside you right now. All you have to do is let it shine. Here's how:

- Remember each and every day to be happy. It's a simple decision.
- No matter how busy you are, invest a few moments every day to remember what you have to be happy about.
- Be in the Now. Now – is your point of personal power. Be happy Now. Find something in this precise moment to be happy about.
- Find memories and feelings that connect you with your happiness. What does it feel like? Where in your body do you feel it?
- Do something that makes you feel happy every day. We can all learn to be far more content within

ourselves; with who we are and what we have.
Decide to be happy right now.

Appreciation and Gratitude – refer to page 30

Love

When you truly love yourself you unlock the potential
for others to love you.

The following suggestions might require a leap of faith
on your part. That's OK. When you are ready, you might
give these ideas a go:

- Mentally send yourself love on a daily basis and
  imagine receiving this love throughout your whole
  body. Give this love your favourite colour, a sound
  or a feeling. Imagine being embraced by this love.
- Mentally send love to others. Sincerely thinking and
  doing things for others is another way to lift our
  spirits.

Give this a go as part of your daily routine:

Imagine that there is an abundance of love in the
World, plenty for all. Because there is. Your whole mind
and body are embraced by this love. After just a few
moments, each and every cell in your body is tenderly
infused with this love. Relish in it. For as long as you wish.
This is the start of new beginnings, of many wondrous

things about to happen, now, when you are ready, imagine sending bundles of love to your friends and family. Notice their eyes light up with joy and happiness as they receive your love and feel the love coming right back at you from these wonderful people in your life. All is well in your world. You live in a loving, supportive and abundant Universe. Tell yourself "I am a loving and lovable person".

Chapter 8

Balancing Your Wheel of Life

The techniques within Moving On UP so far, are designed to help you bring about inner happiness and inner balance.

Along with creating inner balance we can help ourselves to create a state of external balance in our lives by using a simple yet very effective technique called 'The Wheel of Life'.

Like the Mood Tracker, the Wheel of Life is a snapshot. Whereas the Mood Tracker is a snapshot of where we are with our emotions, the Wheel of Life is a snapshot of how fulfilled we are in specific areas of our lives.

The Wheel of Life helps us to quickly identify what's off balance. Zero being the lowest – closest to the centre of the wheel and ten being the highest, at the end of the spoke. Imagine that in all areas of your life you had an eight. When you spin your Wheel of Life, it will spin smoothly. If a specific area in your life is much higher or lower than the rest, your life could be out of balance and the wheel will not spin smoothly. By focusing time and energy on any out of balance areas you can bring your life back into balance.

Now, number each of the eight areas to determine

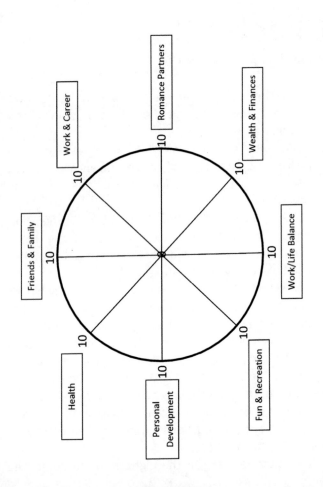

whether you have a wonky wheel or a balanced one!

For example: Consider your health – how happy/content are you with this area of your life? If you think that you would like to improve your health but it is pretty good at the moment, give it a 7, say. If you are extremely happy and there is no room for improvement then give this a 10.

Which areas of your life are currently contributing to a bumpy ride in life? What will your life be like when you are riding smoothly? We can all learn to spin a different Wheel of Life. If you don't yet believe you can, go back to the chapter on changing beliefs in Chapter 6 and carry out the changing beliefs strategy.

Date each wheel and once you have rated each area of your life, carry out the following two step process for each area.

1. In the appreciation column on the next page, enter as many things as possible that you are grateful for in that area of your life. You will find that once you remember one thing, others will flow quickly and easily like a chain reaction. Write them all down.

2. For the purposes of this exercise ignore what you perceive to be realistic. Just take the time to imagine and dream. And now imagine for each of the areas how you want your life to be. Write this up in the present tense as if you are doing it today.

Describe in exquisite detail in the goals column what you will see, hear and feel when you are living this life.

For example:

Life Area	Appreciation	Goals – in present tense
Health	You can make up your own which are specific to you, just as examples; • I appreciate that I can use my senses. • I am grateful that I can walk. • I am grateful that I am self-reliant in certain areas of my life. • I am grateful that I am at xx on the Up Scale	You can make your own which are specific to you, just as examples; • I love the walks that I go on in the Forest • I am fit and am filled with vitality and energy, and I know that the good foods I eat nurture me well. • I nurture my mind with good thoughts and exquisite pictures and am happy and upbeat with myself and life in general.

Live the dream in the movies of your mind. What we think in our minds, we create in our reality. Remember that your mind doesn't know whether something is real or imagined. So when we imagine a great life, our minds will create the same happy chemicals as if we are living that great life. We might as well do this –there's nothing to lose and everything to gain.

Go back to assessing your wheel of life regularly (say every six months) and notice how much the various areas of your life have improved. Plan where you'd like to focus your time and attention in the following months.

When you look back at your wheels of life, you will notice how much more upbeat and happy you are, how much you're moving on up and how smoothly your life runs.

Personal Message

My deepest desire in writing this book has been to share practical techniques and strategies that help you, as much, if not more than they have helped me.

I sincerely hope that this book empowers you to make permanent changes in your life.

To Move UP in life, takes commitment on your part. To embed permanent upbeat habits takes regular repetition.

By adopting these quick and easy techniques, every day, you become more and more in command of your emotions, and your life.

You really do have the inner strength to make lasting improvements to the way you feel. You will be pleasantly surprised at how quickly and easily out-dated thoughts and habits are replaced by new, supportive ones. And from this, you will notice how much more upbeat you feel about yourself and life in general.

Carry Moving on Up around with you and periodically refer to it. Most of all, enjoy it. Each time you remind yourself and do anything from these pages, you increase the likelihood that being Upbeat is your default setting.

Do let me know how you are getting on. I would love to hear from you, you can contact me through my website movingonupnitasaini.com.

With Love

Nita

Quick Reference Guides
Upbeat Boost

1. Accept the reality of your situation.
2. Accept that you, and nobody else, is responsible for your life and its events. You have all the power within you to make changes and improvements.
3. Remember that "This too will pass".
4. Is this matter going to be so important in a month or a years time?
5. Breathe deeply three times, exhaling negative thoughts and emotions and inhaling calmness and clarity.
6. You can decide to either: **C**hange, **A**void or change the way you **F**eel about the situation.
7. Notice any thoughts you have, pictures you are making, or feelings you have relating to this situation. How are any of the pictures, sounds and feelings contributing to you feeling downbeat. Refer to chapter six.
8. Appreciation. Focus on what is working well in your life.
9. BETOP. Believe Everything Turns Out Perfectly.
10. Decide to be upbeat Now.

Up Foundations for Life

- **Go for a Walk**
  20 minutes a day.

- **Smile More**
  One minute at least five times a day.

- **Get a Good Night's Sleep**

- **Breathe Deeply**
  Exhale and inhale deeply three times a day. Ten repetitions.

- **Drink Water**
  1.5-2 litres a day. Make water your preferred daily drink.

Sample Gratitude List

- I am grateful for my family.
- I am grateful for my friends and neighbours.
- I am grateful for the time I spend with my partner, friends and family.
- I am grateful for the hugs that I give and receive.
- I am grateful for my pets.
- I am grateful for the kind words that I receive and give to others.
- I am grateful for the paid and non-paid support that I receive from others.
- I am grateful for the support I give to others.
- I am grateful for enjoyable experiences.
- I am grateful for who I am.
- I am grateful for my senses and what they allow me to do, from being able to listen to birds in the morning, to watching a sunset, to the food that I taste.
- I am grateful for my current physical wellbeing
- I am grateful for my intellect.
- I am grateful for my education.
- I am grateful for the leisure activities I do.
- I am grateful for the food I eat.
- I am grateful for the clothes that I wear.
- I am grateful for my home.
- I am grateful for the warm shower/baths I have.

- I am grateful for the good night's sleep I have.
- I am grateful for my warm bed.
- I am grateful for my existing job and/or past jobs and what they have done for me.

Add other people/experiences/objects that you are grateful for in the spaces below.

....
....
....
....
....
....
....
....
....

To be used in conjunction with "Moving on Up: Secrets to an Upbeat and Happy Life.
www.movingonupnitasaini.com

Daily Upbeat Success Journal

Print out multiple copies of this use one sheet per day to record your daily progress. Copies are available on the website movingonupnitasaini.com . Over time, you will notice how well you have done.

Date.....................

1. Today on a scale of 0 to 10, I feel …	Insert number here ....
2. Up Foundations	o I went for a walk o I remembered to smile more o I slept well o I remembered to breathe deeply o I drank water

3.   Daily Start Reminders
  o   I got physical today by ….
 	
  o   I nurtured myself by….
 	
  o   I indulged myself by….
 	
  o   I ate good mood foods
 	
  o   I kept my good sleep routine
 	
  o   I am grateful for….
	List activities below

o What I am looking forward to in my future, tomorrow, next week, next month....	
4. Positive thoughts I had today were...	
5. Positive pictures I saw today were...	
6. Positive feelings I had today were...	

Make comments here about any other activities that contributed to you feeling more upbeat

....

....

....

....

....

Make comments here about any other activities that contributed to you feeling more upbeat

....
....
....
....

Moving On Up